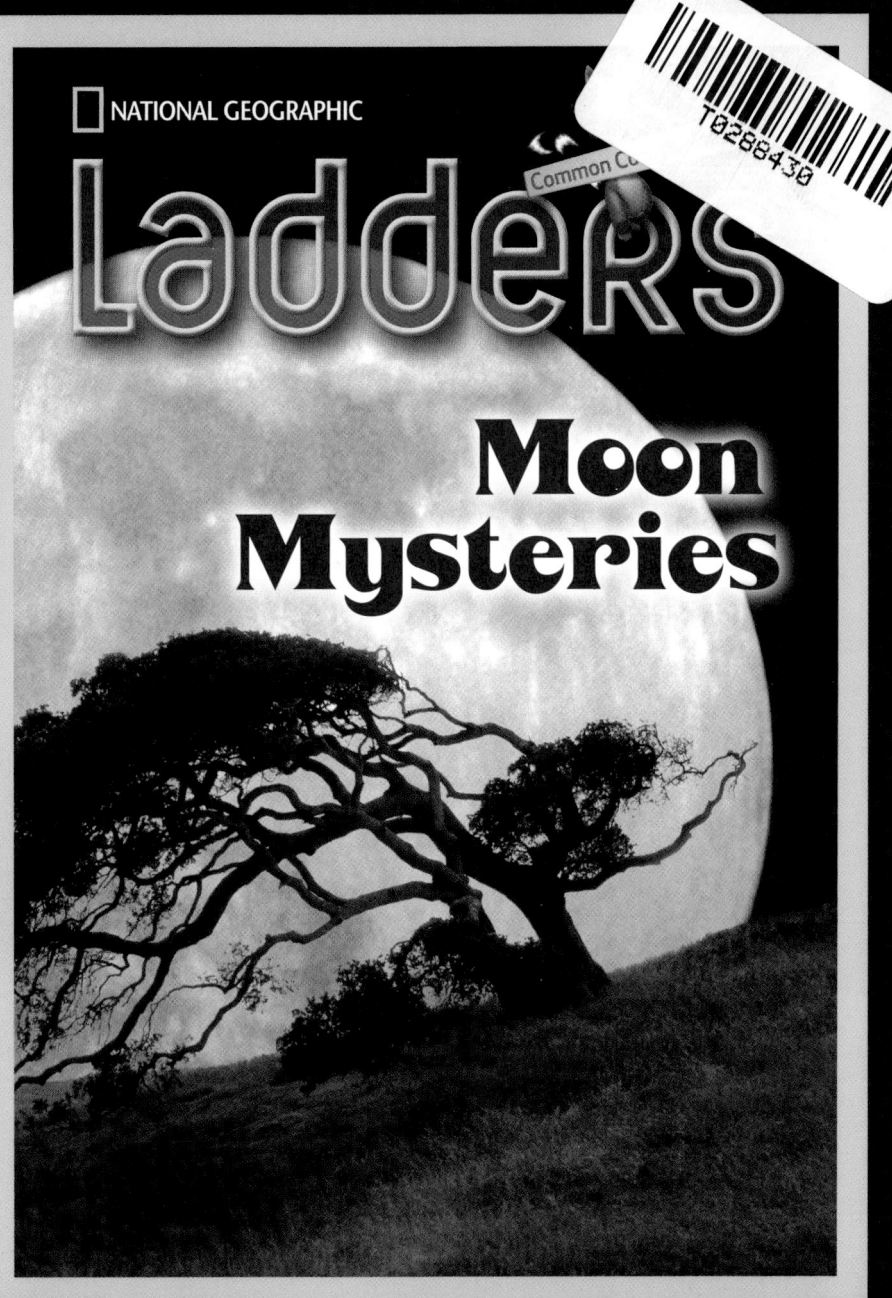

NATIONAL GEOGRAPHIC

Ladders

Moon Mysteries

The Sock Sneak Mystery

by Renee Biermann
illustrated by Laura Perez

NARRATOR 1

NARRATOR 2

ANDRE
male summer camper

TYLER
male summer camper

LUCIA
female summer camper

GRACE
female summer camper

EMMA
female camp counselor

JASPER
male camp counselor

WES
male camp counselor

INTRODUCTION

[**SETTING** *The play takes place at Black Lake Summer Camp.*
NARRATOR 1 and NARRATOR 2 enter and speak to the audience.
They both show excitement.]

NARRATOR 1: Welcome to Black Lake Summer Camp!

NARRATOR 2: This summer, something amazing happened
that had never happened before.

NARRATOR 1: Someone solved a very dark mystery.

NARRATOR 2: What mystery, you ask? A very dark,
sneaky mystery, indeed.

NARRATOR 1 and **NARRATOR 2:** [*look at each other,*
then say together] The mystery of the Sock Sneak!

NARRATOR 1: What's a Sock
Sneak, you ask??

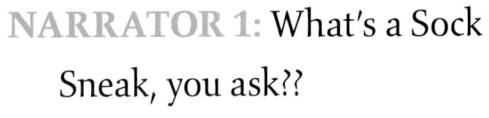

NARRATOR 2: A Sock Sneak is a sneaky person who steals socks.

NARRATOR 1: Why would someone steal socks?

NARRATOR 2: Socks are stolen for FUN! Each year, a counselor at Black Lake Summer Camp steals socks from the campers.

NARRATOR 1: For many years, no one knew who the Sock Sneak was.

NARRATOR 2: The campers never knew when the Sock Sneak would strike, so there was an annual competition to see who could figure it out.

NARRATOR 1: All of that changed this year, however, when a certain clue shed light on the mystery . . . by not shedding light!

NARRATOR 2: Let's see how it all started . . .

ACT 1

[**SETTING** *At Black Lake Summer Camp, EMMA, JASPER, and WES are standing in front of the campers. ANDRE, LUCIA, GRACE, and TYLER are sitting nearby, listening with interest.*]

JASPER: Listen up, campers! It's time for the annual Sock Sneak Competition.

EMMA: [*teasing*] I don't know, guys. We've seen quite a few socks run up the flagpole over the years.

WES: It's true, campers. At some phase during your two-week stay, one of us will steal your socks and run them up the flagpole. It's your job to figure out when this will happen.

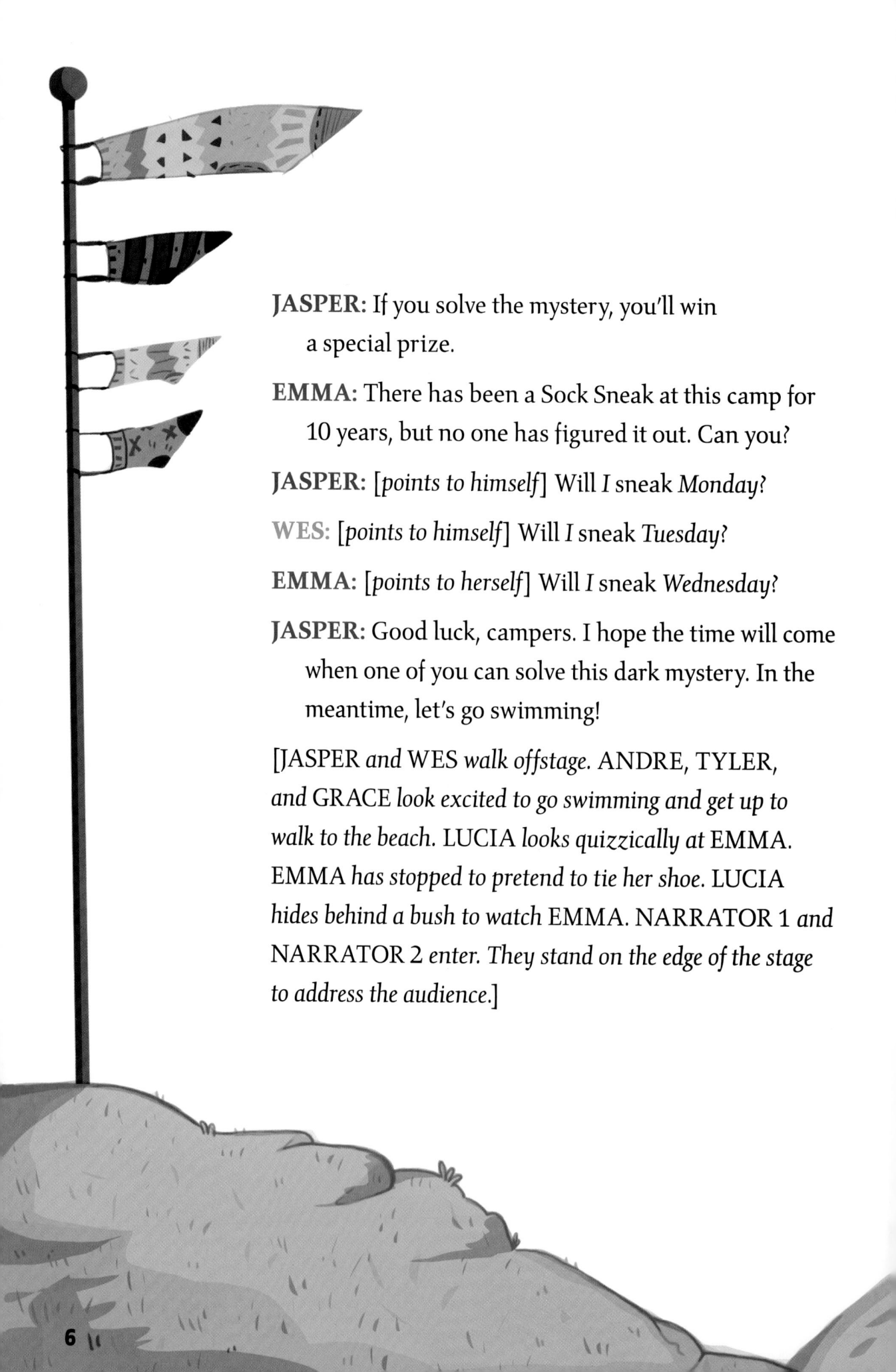

JASPER: If you solve the mystery, you'll win a special prize.

EMMA: There has been a Sock Sneak at this camp for 10 years, but no one has figured it out. Can you?

JASPER: [*points to himself*] Will I sneak *Monday?*

WES: [*points to himself*] Will I sneak *Tuesday?*

EMMA: [*points to herself*] Will I sneak *Wednesday?*

JASPER: Good luck, campers. I hope the time will come when one of you can solve this dark mystery. In the meantime, let's go swimming!

[JASPER *and* WES *walk offstage.* ANDRE, TYLER, *and* GRACE *look excited to go swimming and get up to walk to the beach.* LUCIA *looks quizzically at* EMMA. EMMA *has stopped to pretend to tie her shoe.* LUCIA *hides behind a bush to watch* EMMA. NARRATOR 1 *and* NARRATOR 2 *enter. They stand on the edge of the stage to address the audience.*]

NARRATOR 1: Lucia saw Emma lean down to tie her shoe, but it was already laced.

NARRATOR 2: What was Emma doing? Lucia wanted to find out!

NARRATOR 1: Lucia's friends went to the beach, but she waited behind a bush to see what Emma would do next.

NARRATOR 2: [*looks at NARRATOR 1*] Lucia is very clever.

NARRATOR 1: [*looks at NARRATOR 2 and nods*] Yes, very clever.

[EMMA *stands up. She pulls a piece of folded paper from her pocket and reads it.*]

EMMA: [*speaking to herself*] Hmm . . . . That's right!

[LUCIA *looks confused. She's still watching from behind the bush.* EMMA *goes to put the piece of paper back in her pocket, but she drops it. As* EMMA *walks away,* LUCIA *runs out and snatches the paper.*]

NARRATOR 1: Lucia didn't know what was on that piece of paper, but she thought it could be a clue.

NARRATOR 2: She was correct.

LUCIA: [*speaking to herself*] Very sneaky!

[LUCIA *looks happy and runs to catch up with her friends at the beach.*]

ACT 2

[**SETTING** It's later that night, and the campers have gathered to talk.]

GRACE: I really want to win the Sock Sneak Competition, but I don't know when the Sneak will strike.

ANDRE: I feel the same way. Every year, I try to guess, but I'm always wrong.

TYLER: It'll probably be sometime next week. That's my guess.

LUCIA: [*confident*] I know when the Sock Sneak will strike.

GRACE: What's your guess?

LUCIA: It's not a guess, I figured it out. I know when it will happen.

TYLER: [*doubtful*] Oh yeah, Lucia? When?

LUCIA: It's going to happen tonight.

[TYLER, ANDRE, *and* GRACE
look surprised.]

TYLER: Tonight?

LUCIA: Yes, tonight, and it's going to be Emma!

ANDRE: No way!

GRACE: How do you know?

LUCIA: I'll give you a little clue. It has to do with
  something "**waxing.**"

TYLER: Is someone waxing the dining room floor?

ANDRE: Is someone waxing the camp bus?

LUCIA: [*laughs*] No. Here is another clue. It has to do with something "**waning.**"

GRACE: Did you say "raining"? It's not raining.

LUCIA: [*smiling at GRACE*] No, silly. I said "WANING."

[GRACE, TYLER, *and* ANDRE *all look hopelessly confused.*]

LUCIA: Think about it carefully. There has to be some kind of pattern that the Sock Sneak follows.

TYLER: So the Sock Sneak would do the same thing each year?

ANDRE: Yeah, there has to be a pattern.

GRACE: [*angry*] I still don't know what this has to do with raining because it's not raining!

LUCIA: [*amused*] Oh, Grace, I'm not talking about the weather. Come on. I'll show you.

ACT 3

[**SETTING** *Pathway near the flagpole. GRACE, LUCIA, ANDRE, and TYLER are hiding behind the bushes waiting for EMMA. They are cramped together and are all peeking toward the path.*]

GRACE: Why are we hiding in the bushes?

LUCIA: We're going to catch Emma the Sock Sneak.

ANDRE: Are you sure she's coming?

TYLER: [*frustrated*] Shhh! We don't want anyone to hear us.

[TYLER *moves closer to the group and steps on* GRACE'S *foot.*]

GRACE: Ouch, Tyler, you're standing on my foot!

TYLER: Sorry, Grace!

ANDRE: Quiet!

GRACE: It's so dark out here. I'm scared.

ANDRE: Don't be afraid, Grace. We're all here together, so you'll be OK.

GRACE: I still don't know why we're here. Let's go back to the campfire.

TYLER: No. We have to see if Lucia was right. Shhh!

[EMMA *walks quietly down the path to the flagpole with her arms filled with socks.*]

LUCIA: I told you! Here she comes. Let's surprise her.

ANDRE: Let's jump out on the count of three. One . . . two . . . three!

[LUCIA, GRACE, TYLER, *and* ANDRE *jump out from behind the bushes. They turn on their flashlights and shine them at* EMMA.]

LUCIA: We got you, Sock Sneak!

TYLER: SURPRISE!

ANDRE: SURPRISE!

GRACE: SURPRISE!

[EMMA *jumps in surprise and the socks go flying out of her hands.*]

EMMA: [*surprised*] ACK! [*laughs*] I've finally been discovered!

[*Everyone laughs.* LUCIA, GRACE, TYLER, *and* ANDRE *help* EMMA *pick up the socks.*]

EMMA: Which one of you figured it out?

ANDRE: It was Lucia.

GRACE: I still don't understand what this has to do with "waxing" or "raining" . . . I mean "waning."

LUCIA: Those clues were about the **lunar** calendar. The moon has **phases,** and it can be waxing or waning.

TYLER: But tonight's a **new moon,** so we cannot see it!

LUCIA: I know. That's how I knew tonight would be the night the Sock Sneak struck. When there's a new moon, it's very dark outside.

GRACE: I understand now! The Sock Sneak strikes when there's a new moon so that no one can see her!

LUCIA: Exactly! I saw Emma drop this piece of paper today.

[LUCIA *pulls out piece of paper and unfolds it. It's a lunar calendar for July.*]

LUCIA: Today is the new moon. [*points to new moon on calendar*] I knew Emma would be at the flagpole tonight because it would be so dark.

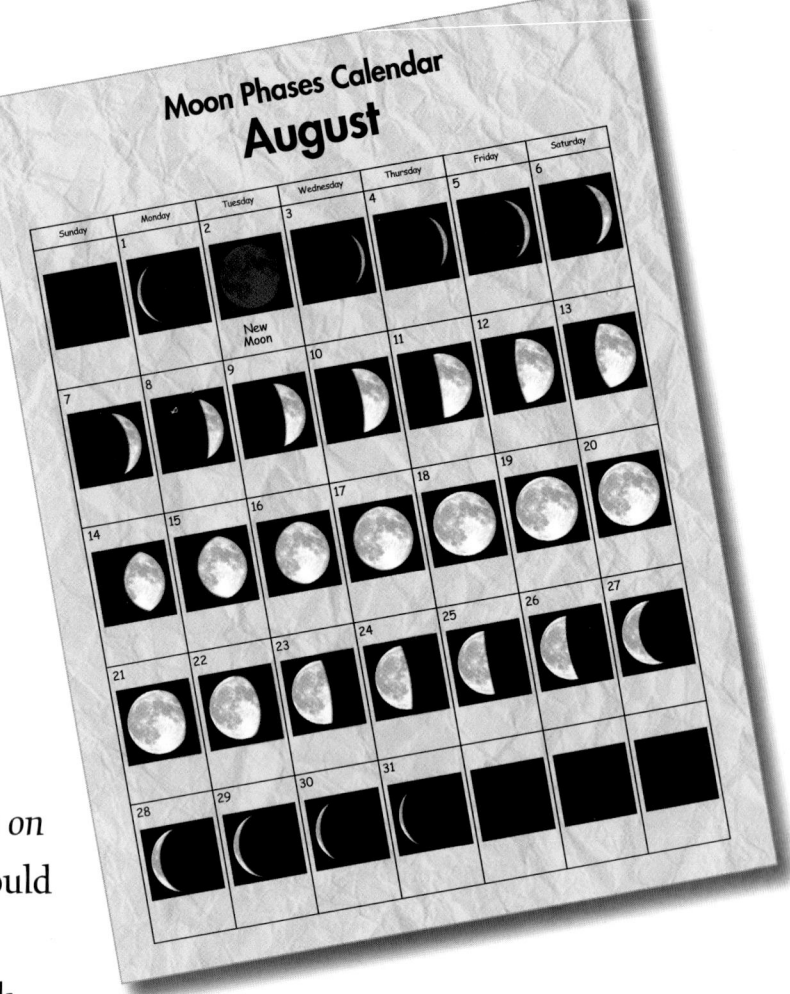

EMMA: I'm so proud of you, Lucia. Good job! You win the prize!

[EMMA *pulls a special, colorful flag out of her pocket. She takes a marker and writes "LUCIA" on the flag. Then she runs the flag up the flagpole.*]

[JASPER *and* WES *come running up to the flagpole.*]

JASPER: [*worried*] What's all the commotion about?

WES: [*anxious*] We heard you yelling!

EMMA: Everyone is fine. Lucia caught me sneaking out here with the socks!

[*Everyone cheers.*]

[NARRATOR 1 *and* NARRATOR 2 *enter.*]

NARRATOR 1: And that is how the Sock Sneak mystery was solved at Black Lake Summer Camp.

NARRATOR 2: The end.

[NARRATOR 1 *and* NARRATOR 2 *bow.*]

Check In How does Lucia solve the mystery?

Read to find out why the shape of the moon appears to change.

OBSERVING THE MOON

by Nate George

Moon, Earth, and Sun

The moon is a **sphere,** or a ball, that constantly **revolves,** or travels around, Earth. One complete revolution around Earth takes about one month. As the moon is revolving around Earth, both Earth and the moon are also revolving around the sun.

The moon may look bright in the sky, but it does not give off its own light. It reflects light from the sun. The "moonlight" you see is sunlight that has bounced off the moon.

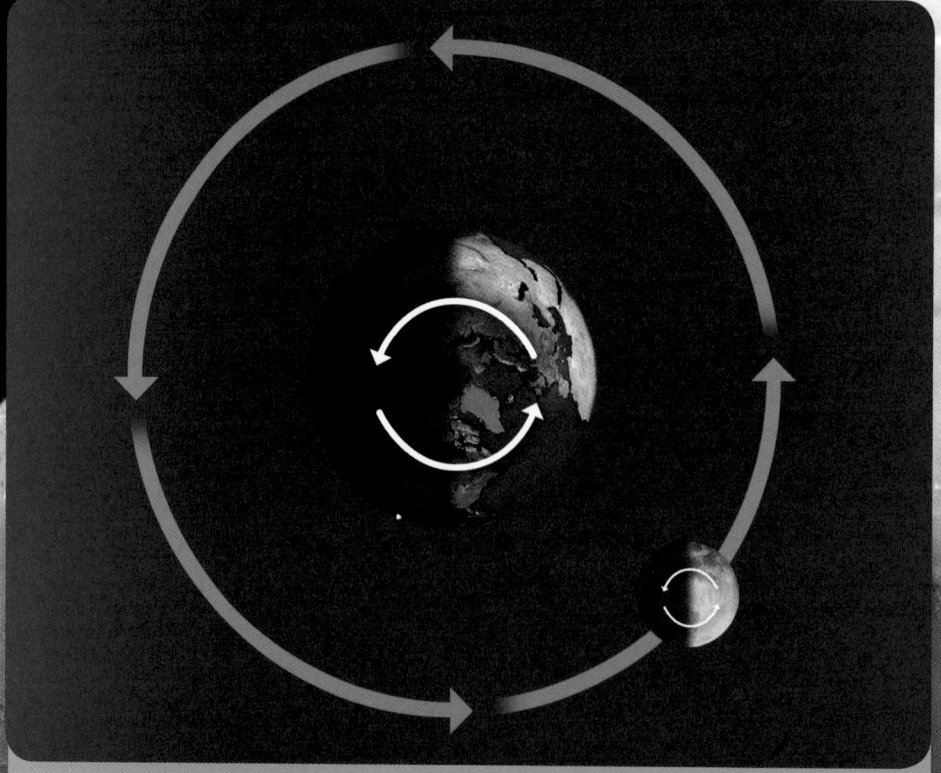

The blue arrows show that the moon revolves around Earth.
The white arrows show that Earth and the moon also rotate, or spin.

A **full moon** occurs when Earth is positioned between the sun and the moon. During a full moon, you can see the entire sunlit half of the moon. If you are facing a full moon, where will the sun be?

A **new moon** occurs when the moon is positioned between the sun and Earth. During a new moon, you can't see any of the sunlit half of the moon.

Full moon

New moon

Phases of the Moon

Suppose you want to describe the moon. You could say it looks like a circle, a half circle, or even like a banana, and each description would be correct because the shape of the moon seems to change over time. Each shape is a **phase** of the moon.

The sun lights the half of the moon that faces it. As the moon revolves around Earth, you see the different parts of the lighted half. Sometimes you see all of it—that's a full moon. Sometimes you see only part of the lighted half—that could be a crescent moon, a quarter moon, or a gibbous moon. Sometimes you don't see any of it—that's a new moon.

The phases change in a predictable pattern. When the moon is **waxing,** you see more and more of its lighted half. When the moon is **waning,** you see less and less of it. The time from one new moon to the next new moon is about one month.

Phases of the Moon

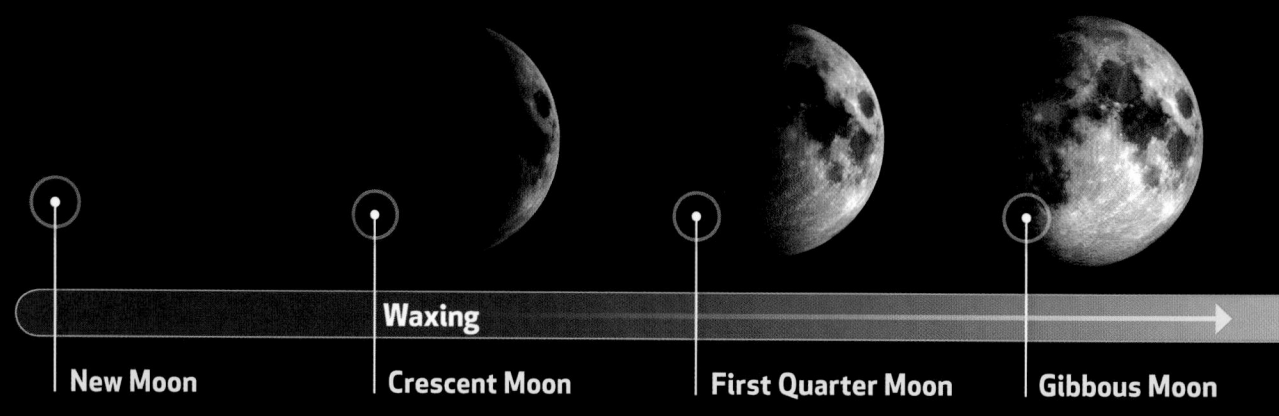

Waxing

New Moon | Crescent Moon | First Quarter Moon | Gibbous Moon

Why a Quarter Moon?

During the first quarter moon phase, the moon looks like half of a circle. So you may wonder why this phase is called a *quarter moon*. Remember, the moon revolves around Earth. When you see the moon in this phase, it has completed one quarter of its revolution. That's the reason this phase is called a *quarter moon*.

The moon can be seen sometimes during the day and sometimes at night.

Full Moon

Waning

Gibbous Moon

Last Quarter Moon

Crescent Moon

Lunar Eclipses

A **lunar eclipse** occurs when Earth's shadow falls on the moon. Remember that a full moon occurs only when Earth is between the sun and the moon. Full moons are usually a little above or a little below Earth's shadow. However, a full moon can sometimes be directly in line with Earth and the sun. If that happens, the moon falls in Earth's shadow—causing a lunar eclipse. Use the diagram to help you observe what happens during a lunar eclipse.

You might think that the moon would disappear from view during a lunar eclipse, but instead, its color changes from dusty gray to dark red.

A total lunar eclipse occurs when Earth's shadow falls on the entire lighted half of the moon. A partial lunar eclipse occurs when only a part of the lighted half of the moon is darkened.

In this diagram, we are looking "down," as if from above the North Pole. Match the letters in the diagram to each photo of the moon below. Look at how Earth's shadow covers the moon in each photo. Notice that the moon is not completely dark during an eclipse. Its color changes from gray to red.

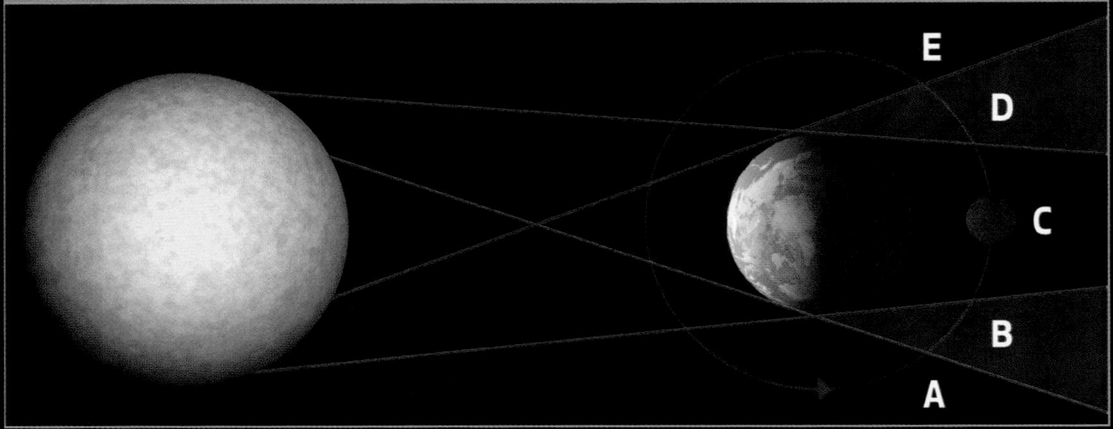

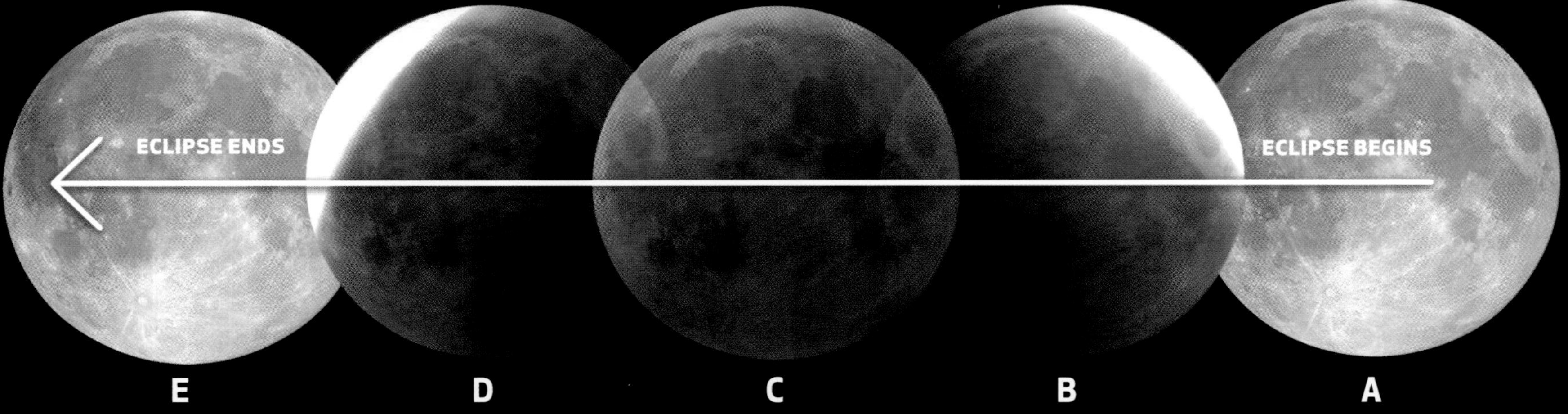

ECLIPSE BEGINS

A   B   C   D   E

ECLIPSE ENDS

Check In   How is a lunar eclipse different from a phase of the moon?

GENRE **Folk Tale** **Read to find out** what this folk tale tries to explain.

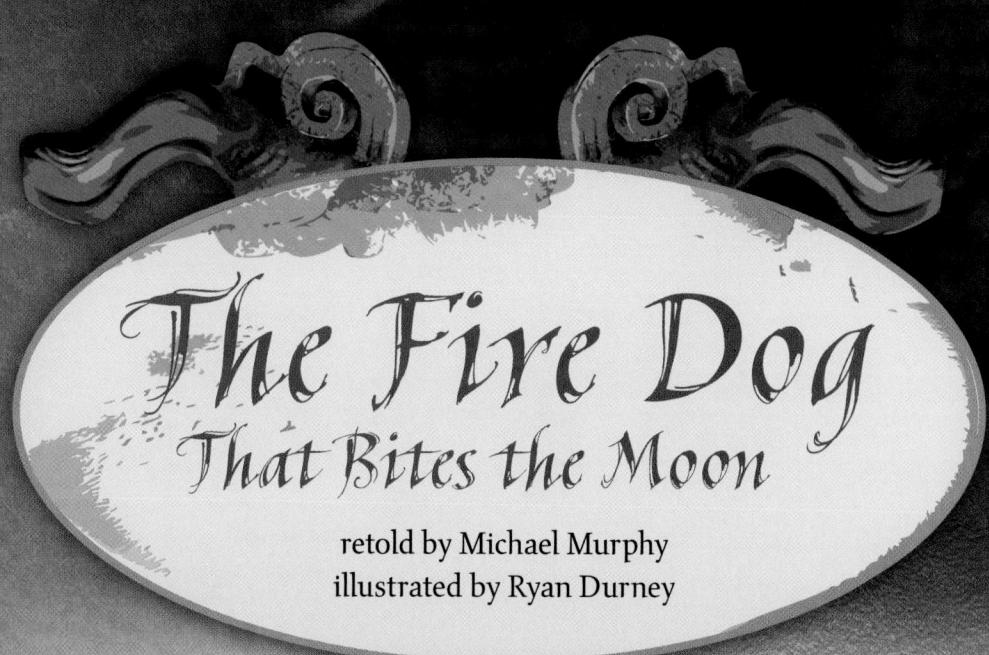

The Fire Dog
That Bites the Moon

retold by Michael Murphy
illustrated by Ryan Durney

The moon has mystified people for ages. Some people in the past created folk tales as a way to explain things they didn't understand about the moon, such as the **phases** of the moon when it **waxes** and **wanes** or why the moon is dark during a **new moon.** This Korean tale is one explanation of a partial lunar eclipse.

Long, long ago, in an underground country of **caverns** called Gamag Nara, the Land of Darkness, the only light was firelight. Inhabitants of the caverns had enormous Fire Dogs. These dogs had great strength and agility and helped the people carry huge sticks and logs to keep their fires burning.

The king became more and more concerned that, even with the great fires, his cavernous country was too dark. The king heard tales of great lights, the sun and the moon, in the sky above Earth. He wondered, could a Fire Dog capture one of those lights for the Land of Darkness?

The king **summoned** his fiercest Fire Dog from its den in the depths of his kingdom. He ordered the dog to leap into the sky, **seize** the sun, and bring it back to light the Land of Darkness. So the dog raced like the wind through the long, winding caverns and reached the exit of the Land of Darkness, where light from above streamed in through a large opening.

Then the fiercest Fire Dog made a gigantic leap. Higher and higher into the bright sky it flew. Closer and closer to the hot sun it went. But then, lo and behold, the fiercest Fire Dog of all realized that it could go no farther. Although it did its best to do what it had been ordered to do, it could not get close enough to the sun to steal it; it was just too hot. So the fiercest Fire Dog had no choice but to return to the caverns of the Land of Darkness without the light that the king wanted for his kingdom.

The king did not give up. He knew that the moon would not bring as much light to the Land of Darkness as the sun would bring, but he decided that moonlight would be better than firelight alone. So he summoned his next-fiercest Fire Dog from the depths of his cavernous kingdom, ordered it to leap into the sky, seize the moon, and bring it back to the Land of Darkness.

So the second-fiercest Fire Dog made a gigantic leap. Higher and higher into the night sky it flew. Closer and closer to the moon it went. Then, lo and behold, it was able to reach the moon!

But, alas, when the king's second-fiercest Fire Dog tried to bite the moon, it was so cold that it froze the dog's mouth! Even so, the Fire Dog was **tenacious.** It bit the moon once. It bit the moon twice. And then it bit the moon again and again, each time swallowing more and more of the moon.

But in the end, the Fire Dog was forced to spit the moon out. And so the second-fiercest Fire Dog had no choice but to return to the caverns of the Land of Darkness without the light that the king wanted for his kingdom.

Despite these two failed attempts to seize light and bring it back to the Land of Darkness, the king never gave up hope.

The king continued to send his second-fiercest Fire Dog above ground and ordered it to steal the moon as a way of bringing light into his cavernous kingdom. Unfortunately, the tenacious Fire Dog never had any success despite its repeated efforts. It always had to spit out the ice-cold moon after biting it, and so the Land of Darkness remained as dark as ever, and the king's wish remained unfulfilled.

From that day forward, people above ground have told the story of the Fire Dog that bites the moon . . . and how the part of the moon that looks dark during a lunar eclipse is the bite of the tenacious Fire Dog.

Check In How does this folk tale explain a partial lunar eclipse?

Discuss | Text Structure and Concepts

1. Explain the differences between a play and a story. What elements does a play have that a story does not have?

2. How do the visuals in the folk tale help tell the story?

3. What is happening when there is a full moon? Explain.

4. What is happening when there is a new moon? Explain.

5. What questions do you still have about moon phases and eclipses? What else would you like to know?